51 Secrets of Motherhood

(That Your Mother Never Told You)

51 Secrets of Motherhood

(That Your Mother Never Told You)

For Moms-To-Be,
From Rebecca Matthias,

the woman who dresses 2.7 million
expectant moms each year.

Franklin Mason Press
Trenton, New Jersey

Dedicated to my mother, Wilma,
my own source of strength.

Visit 51secrets.motherhood.com

ISBN 0-9760469-0-3
Library of Congress Control Number: 2004115375
Copyright © Rebecca Matthias, 2005
Photo Copyright © Paula Funari, 2005
www.paulafunari.com

Editorial Staff: Lisa Willever, Marcia Jacobs, Brooks Spencer
Cover and Book Design: Peri Poloni, Knockout Design
www.knockoutbooks.com

Printed in Italy
Published in the United States of America
Franklin Mason Press, Trenton, New Jersey
www.franklinmasonpress.com

Franklin Mason Press and Motherhood® Maternity are pleased
to support and promote the valuable work of the March of Dimes,
by donating 25 cents for each book sold to its cause as well as
information contained on page 111.

The March of Dimes does not endorse specific brands or products. The opinions expressed
in this publication are those of the individual author(s) and may not reflect March of Dimes
policies. Information included in this publication does not take the place of guidance from
your health care provider. Always verify information with your health care provider.

While reasonable care has been taken during the preparation of this edition, neither the
publisher, editors, author, or contributing authors can accept any responsibility for any con-
sequences arising from the use thereof or from the information contained therein.

From Rebecca Matthias

Hi, my name is Rebecca Matthias and I have spent the past 23 years dressing pregnant women. I may have seen you in one of the many stores that are part of my company's collection of maternity boutiques. I have been listening to you, thinking about you, and sharing your hopes, dreams, and fears. I believe I have the best job in the world because I am invited to share in the lives of over 2.7 million pregnant women who shop in my stores every year. As a mother of three myself, I have experienced what you are experiencing, and I know that this is the most amazing nine months of a woman's life. I also know that you could easily spend your entire pregnancy reading many of the hundreds of books on the subject. This book will not require a trimester to read, but on the contrary, provide you with some great advice for your mind, body, and spirit and still leave you time to *enjoy this magical transformation*.

While pregnancy changes every woman to varying degrees, for me, being pregnant is what started my own odyssey. Determined to create maternity clothing that reflected the style of real women, I built a company called Mothers Work®. I fell in love with the whole experience of being pregnant, and I started a little mail order catalog business selling maternity clothes. My mail order business developed into a chain of stores, and then three chains. Today, my company sells over $500 million of maternity clothes, every year, through our 1,100 locations called *A Pea in the Pod*®, *Mimi Maternity*®, and *Motherhood*® *Maternity*. There are about four million births each year in the United States, and six out of every ten pregnant women shop in one of my stores. So, over the last 23 years, as I have traveled the country and spoken to you, I have immersed myself in the world of moms-to-be.

As I speak to pregnant women, I hear many of the same questions, hopes, and fears. I find myself saying things like 'you are not alone if you're thrilled and terrified at the same time.' And while I share my own experiences, I am also learning from all of you. Writing this book has become my way of sharing what I have learned along the way.

I have invited **Dr. Robert Siefring, OB/GYN**, to share what he has learned in his 20+ years in the field. He is a wonderful doctor as well as a member of the faculty at Rutgers University. He has delivered thousands and thousands of babies and counseled as many moms-to-be. His dedication to expectant moms, goes beyond the medical and physical issues of pregnancy, and his patients know that no question or concern is crazy.

Since pregnancy is as much a spiritual experience as a physical experience, I am grateful that **Deepak Chopra** and his daughter, **Mallika Chopra**, have contributed their timeless wisdom. As the spiritual connoisseur of the world, Deepak Chopra, has offered his insight to the spiritual side of this life-changing event. The author of dozens of books, including his holistic, mind and body approach to pregnancy, *Magical Beginnings, Enchanted Lives*, his words are encouraging and uplifting. Mallika Chopra, the mother of two beautiful girls, has recently authored a book for new mothers, entitled **One Hundred Promises To My Baby**.

In addition to my esteemed guest contributors, I have surveyed 1,000 expectant mothers and collected advice and secrets from new moms all over the country. The survey results are scattered throughout the book and a special section called *To New Moms, From New Moms* shares the insight of women who are pregnant or have just given birth. Their humor and strength shine through each contribution and I am honored to share their experiences.

As my youngest child approaches adulthood, I must admit I'm always a little jealous when I speak to moms-to-be. I remember every little detail of those miraculous nine months. I went through it three times, and each time was better than the one before. Sure, I suffered the heartburn, the backaches, the worry, and the secret fears. But how do you describe the feeling of being kicked by your baby-to-be or knowing that you are creating a new life, and just counting the days until your baby is placed in your arms?

Most people think that the nine months of pregnancy are about as much fun as going to the dentist every day. But here's the greatest secret of all — *these are going to be the most fabulous nine months of your life.* You are about to become a mom! You are about to create a life! A few cases of heartburn and a few backaches are trivial compared to the amazing transformation that you are engineering.

If I see you as I travel around the country, it will be an honor to meet you and discuss a topic I hold near to my heart. As you read through the book, I urge you to jot down some of your own secrets to pass along to someone who is just starting to dream about becoming a mom. And if you have learned any secrets that I have overlooked, please let me know.

Visit 51secrets.motherhood.com

Have a great nine months!

Rebecca

You will be
the star of a show
that runs
approximately
nine months.

Table of Contents

A clever slogan once claimed that the army does more before 6 a.m. than some people do all day. As a mother, you will do twice that amount before the army even wakes up!

~ 1 ~
Welcome to the
Secret Society of Motherhood

You encounter them every day. You think you know them. You read about them. You hear them talking to each other, but you aren't privy to the Secrets until you become one of them — a mother, that is. You can read about the joy and the pain of Motherhood, but until you are up all night with a sick baby, you can never know how excruciating the pain is. And the first time your newborn gives you that little, milky smile, you will know joy that you have never felt before.

I can tell you all about it, but you won't truly understand it until you pass through the doors of this *Secret Society*. Nature has given you nine months to be an acolyte before you are sworn in. Once you are initiated, there is never any resigning.

The next 50 secrets are your first glimpse into this Secret World you are about to enter.

Welcome!

2

You're About To Turn Into Your Mother! (And that's okay)

Deep down inside, this is every woman's secret fear — turning into your mother. But it is your destiny, so don't fight it. Remember when your mother said, "I don't care if everyone is doing it" or "If everyone jumped off a bridge would you jump, too?" Well, now you will understand that she was right about many things. Now it is your obligation to set your own children on the right path.

My mother once said, "You would cut off your arm for your child, but you won't lift a finger for your mother." Nature has set up a one way chain of benevolence and the best way you re-pay your mother for giving you life and raising you is by passing along your mother's love to your own children. That's why it's okay to turn into your mother, so don't fight it.

3

Two Tickets to Paradise

It may be a while before you and your husband get away for a romantic vacation for two, so TAKE ONE NOW.

When I say "a while", I mean like twenty-five years or so. Even if you do manage to go away together, it really won't be the same. Once you are parents, you will always find plenty to worry about. If the babysitter/mom/ mother-in-law doesn't call you, then believe me, you will be calling her!

An island getaway is a nice idea, but even if that is not financially in the picture, any place that gets you and your partner away together will work. Trust me, you will cherish the memory when you are changing diapers at 1am.

Recipe for a perfect picnic:

a sunny day,
ripe strawberries,
sparkling cider,
time alone.

4

Before Two Became A Few

With the hustle and bustle of preparing for a new baby, be sure you don't neglect your husband. *(I know that all moms-to-be are not married and I support everyone's right to choose their own lifestyle, so skip this one if it does not apply to you.)*

Now, for those of you who are married, once the baby arrives, it is so easy to fall in love with your little one. This is completely natural, but don't forget the one you loved first. Make the time and re-create the romance over and over with your husband, even in the midst of diapers, nursing, and Baby Love.

Remember, when your little precious bundle of joy turns into a surly teenager, your husband will still be there for you if you treat him right along the way.

~ 5 ~

Who's In The Mood?

*In a recent survey of 1,000 pregnant women,
the percentage of couples having sex
in the last week was:*

women in their first trimester: 63%

women in their second trimester: 60%

women in their third trimester: 58%

For a while, you will have to be a bit more creative with the how, and once your baby arrives, you'll need to pay attention to the *where* and the *when!* Don't misinterpret lack of sleep for lack of interest. If you're just too tired, cuddling makes for a close second and will keep you connected until you both find the energy.

Daddy, You're It!

While pregnancy is more physically and emotionally demanding for a mother-to-be, don't overlook the daddy-to-be.

It may seem like you are the parent doing all of the work right now, but your partner is half of this equation. So many women complain that their husbands don't help out enough with the children, but by the time the children are 3 or 4 years old, it is far too late to change his behavior and start including him.

START NOW. Make sure your husband is 100% involved in your pregnancy. Take him shopping for your new wardrobe. Share your doctor's every word. Bring him into the labor and delivery room and let him change the first diaper. Men have a tendency to hold back around *"women's issues"* and may not be great at displaying their emotions, but they are there. Often times, they are just waiting for the invitation. If you nurture your husband, along with your new baby, you will grow a beautiful family, together.

~ 7 ~

Sensational Single Moms

The greatest secret for single moms-to-be: you are not alone!

Let's hear it for single moms-to-be, whether by choice or by circumstance. You will have your own challenges, but in some ways this will make your pregnancy even more special. You are going to have an incredibly strong bond with your new baby. Most importantly, you are not alone. Find your own support group, rely on your friends and family, and mostly, draw upon your own inner strength. It is this strength and this example that will be passed directly to your child.

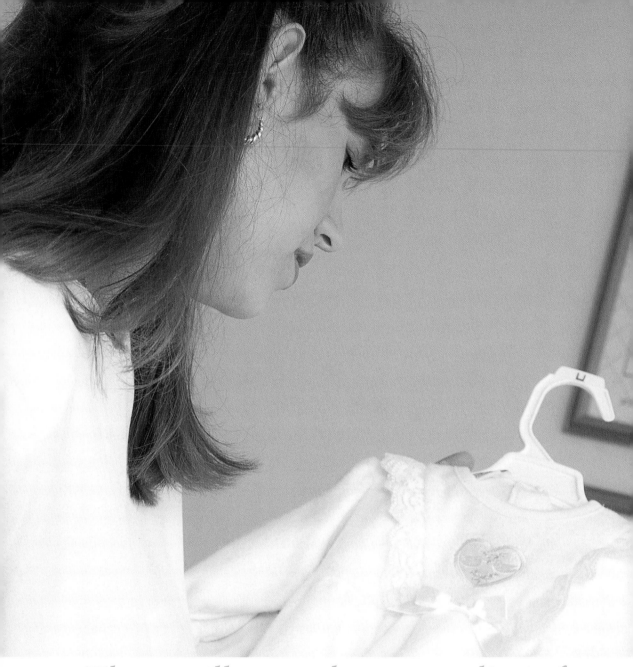

There will never be an age limit for
tea parties, little league,
bedtime kisses, & first steps.

8

The New Age
of Motherhood

The secret is out — there is no "right" time to have a baby. According to the U.S. Department of Health and Human Services, over the last thirty years, the average age of first time moms in the United states has gone from 21.4 years old to 25 years old. This pattern of older first-time moms is also seen in most of the developed countries of the world. In 2000, in Switzerland, for example, the average age of first time moms was 29!

It may not be a co-incidence that, during the last thirty years, more women have pursued educational and career paths. From 1970 to 2000, the number of women completing college has nearly doubled, and the number of women in the labor force has gone up by almost 40 percent.

Many women are simply waiting until the time is right for them. Having a baby in your 30's and 40's is not a rarity anymore and you will probably have the patience, the confidence, and the life perspective to be a superlative mother. While there are greater risks to develop hypertension, diabetes, and genetic defects, today's obstetricians have excellent monitoring capabilities. Older mothers need not look at these pregnancies as mine fields, but as pregnancies with a great potential for success.

While moms in their twenties have the advantage of high energy and great physical condition, the only one who knows which age is right for you, is you.

DEEPAK CHOPRA, M.D.

Author of

Magical Beginnings, Enchanted Lives

A Conscious Pregnancy

Photo by Jeremiah Sullivan

The creative impulse of life is the most powerful force in the universe. Mysterious and inexplicable, it is more substantial than matter, subtler than thought, and more enduring than time. Since the beginning of humanity we have sought explanations of how life emerges from inanimate elements. Despite the unraveling of the genetic code, ife remains as much a mystery now as in ancient times.

The perennial wisdom traditions tell us that archetypal gods and goddesses brought us forth in their image so that we could recreate and honor them in our image. Science ponders the organizing principles that seduce atoms into molecules, molecules into complex biochemicals, and biochemicals into self-replicating systems. Do life forms exist to reproduce DNA molecules or do DNA molecules exist to reproduce life forms? Whether you see the universe as personal or impersonal, from a spiritual or a scientific perspective, you have to marvel at the animating vital force that orchestrates the creation of all living beings.

The universe is recreated in every individual life. Birth and death are merely parentheses in the never-ending story of creation. Each human birth holds the promise of adventure, drama, love, and loss. In the process of creation, the universal ocean of love temporarily flows in rivers of individuality seeking their return to the source. Your baby's conception and birth are the first pages of a new tale — the first steps on her path through this world of infinite possibilities.

Every birth should be a celebration. The magic and the mystery of life's creative process enable each individual and each new generation to recapitulate the entire history of life while seeking ever-new expressions. As your baby takes her first breath and the umbilical cord is cut, she becomes an individual. She separates from your body and formally begins her journey of self-discovery. Intuition and research clearly show us that long before your baby is launched through the birth canal, she has begun exploring her own personhood.

The creative impulse of life is the most powerful force in the universe. Mysterious and inexplicable, it is more substantial than matter, subtler than thought, and more enduring than time. Since the beginning of humanity we have sought explanations of how life emerges from inanimate elements. Despite the unraveling of the genetic code, life remains as much a mystery now as in ancient times.

The perennial wisdom traditions tell us that archetypal gods and goddesses brought us forth in their image so that we could recreate and honor them in our image. Science ponders the organizing principles that seduce atoms into molecules, molecules into complex biochemicals, and biochemicals into self-replicating systems. Do life forms exist to reproduce DNA molecules or do DNA molecules exist to reproduce life forms? Whether you see the universe as personal or impersonal, from a spiritual or a scientific perspective, you have to marvel at the animating vital force that orchestrates the creation of all living beings.

The universe is recreated in every individual life. Birth and death are merely parentheses in the never-ending story of creation. Each human birth holds the promise of adventure, drama, love, and loss. In the process of creation, the universal ocean of love temporarily flows in rivers of individuality seeking their return to the source. Your baby's conception and birth are the first pages of a new tale — the first steps on her path through this world of infinite possibilities.

Every birth should be a celebration. The magic and the mystery of life's creative process enable each individual and each new generation to recapitulate the entire history of life while seeking ever-new expressions. As your baby takes her first breath and the umbilical cord is cut, she becomes an individual. She separates from your body and formally begins her journey of self-discovery. Intuition and research clearly show us that long before your baby is launched through the birth canal she has begun exploring her own personhood.

Your baby's sense of self-awareness dawns early as she grows inside your watery womb. As soon as her sensory awareness develops, she perceives and responds to subtle sounds, sensations, sights, tastes and smells from inside your body. Your interpretations of the world filter through your body to your unborn baby. She readily learns to associate her experiences with feelings and emotions and has pleasures and discomforts of her own. For nine months while your baby is linked to you as her mother ship, she is continually tapping into your database of the world. Your baby learns to associate sensory impulses with feelings and identifies those that bring nourishment and those that feel toxic. Life learning clearly begins before birth.

Feelings and desires are shaped by our intrauterine experiences. Science has demonstrated that every wisp of experience is metabolized into the substance of our minds and bodies, both before and after we are born into this world. Nourishing experiences from conception through life are transformed into healthy bodies and healthy minds, while toxic experiences create unhealthy ones.

Health is not the mere absence of disease; it is a state of physical, psychological, emotional and spiritual well being. We can even go further and define health as a higher state of consciousness, in which we recognize that the same field of intelligence that underlies our life underlies every living being. In a true state of health, we become incapable of hurting others or ourselves. To achieve this state it is important that we feel loved, nourished, secure, contented and happy, right from the beginning. From the moment of conception, the unborn baby experiences the thoughts and actions of her mother. This is because mind and body are inseparably one. Wherever a thought goes, a molecule follows. The impulses in our minds are instantly translated into a palette of neurochemicals. These chemicals communicate with cells and tissues throughout our body. The unborn baby is a part of her mother's body. Therefore, a mother's thoughts, emotions and feelings translate into molecules that enter into the body of her fetus.

You and your baby are continuously sharing each other's molecules and experiences. This dynamic exchange of information and these chemical messengers are the codes of communication between your heart and mind and the heart and mind of your unborn baby. The start of a rich emotional life begins as early as conception. The choices that you make as a mother are key to providing the best beginning, and your expanded awareness is the key to making the best choices. Given this information, there is only one rule that really applies in making choices. Make your choices consciously with one question in mind, "Will the choice I am making this moment expand the experience of love and nurturing in my life, the life of my family, and my baby's life?" If the answer is clearly yes, go ahead and make the choice with passion and finesse. Your baby will grow up to be a person with expanded awareness who could possibly change the world.

Deepak Chopra, M.D.
Author: *Book of Secrets: Unlocking the Hidden Dimensions of Your Life*
Co-author (with David Simon MD): *Magical Beginnings, Enchanted Lives*

9

Soon, It Will All Make Sense

For a lot of women, having a baby answers the question "Why am I here?" Creating a life is such a monumental event, it inspires our spirituality to rise to the surface of our consciousness. For maybe the first time in your life, you feel that you have a huge purpose.

If you weren't particularly religious, you might find yourself thinking back to your upbringing and re-kindling a new interest in your own religion. As you think about bringing up your baby, you may realize that this is an important area that you hadn't thought about for awhile.

Now is the time for you and your husband to agree on your baby's religion. If you have a disagreement on the subject, better to start hashing it out now. Regardless of your beliefs, having a baby will probably be the closest any of us will come to nirvana.

*Pregnancy should never
take away
from who you were,
but add
to who you are.*

The only limits you'll face,
are those you impose upon yourself.

— 10 —

Begin Your New Chapter

Question: *How do I maintain my identity and not lose myself to motherhood?*

Answer: *Motherhood isn't the end of life as you knew it but the beginning of a new chapter in your own continuing story.*

This is a serious question, because it is important to maintain the right balance between baby, husband, and you! After all, you had and should still have, your own goals, dreams, and interests. You don't want to lose them, you want to hold onto to them and make room in your life for your new baby.

While it is easy to get swept up in your new, exciting role, you will be much happier if you make time for yourself. Keep up with the friends you love, the work you do, the hobbies you have — adjusted, of course, to accommodate your new responsibilities.

~ 11 ~

Enjoy Your Pregnancy, *Really*

Contrary to what you may have heard, you will never be as mellow as when you are pregnant. Why, you may ask?

PMS? It's on hold for nine months. Anxiety? Irritability? What's that? You never met a nicer woman than one who is pregnant. It might be because she is dreaming about her baby to be, or it might be because her husband is treating her like a queen, or it might be because she is on a hormone high.

Enjoy it!

12

Now Is The Time To Start A Business

Believe it or not, there is never a better time to start a business than when you have a baby. Women seem to be at their creative best when they are doing the *ultimate in creating*.

Once they have a new baby to contend with, many women enjoy the flexibility they find from starting their own business. They may not be ready to give up their working life altogether, but may also be reluctant to continue a hectic job. Your new business can be as big or small as you make it, and while you may work as hard or harder as an entrepreneur, it will be on your terms, and on your schedule.

Since everything is changing right now anyway, if you have ever thought of starting a business, it's the perfect time to take the plunge.

Start A 529 College Savings Plan

College may seem like a long way off, but this secret is for every expectant parent.

$10 a month, now, will turn into thousands when your baby starts college. New tax rules, called the *529 College Savings Plans,* allow you to start a college fund that is tax advantaged, and therefore grows more than an ordinary savings account.

Regardless of how much money you have or don't have, a minor financial commitment today, can have a major impact on your child's future. When you start a college fund for your baby, you are saying, "I love you and care about your education. I want you to have an independent means of achieving your future goals, whatever you decide them to be."

This one simple act will ensure that your child has the means to shape his or her future. If you can only afford $5 or $10 a month, set it aside. And even if you are very wealthy, you know that things can always change and regardless of your circumstances, you will be able to launch your child into life with an education. How great is that for your baby?

SPECIAL FROM

ROBERT P. SIEFRING, M.D.

Assistant Professor of Obstetrics and Gynecology,
UMDNJ, Robert Wood Johnson Medical School,
Full Time Faculty at Cooper Hospital Medical Center

The most important piece of advice that I can give to parents-to-be is that pregnancies do not follow the published norms found in textbooks, pregnancy manuals, and documentary films. They may bear some resemblance to these observations, however, if a pregnancy is not following the observations verbatim, this does not mean there is a problem or there is an abnormality.

Information, found in books or other resources, is meant to be a guideline, not an absolute rule. It is more important to be able to relax, be flexible, and try to take things as they come. In addition, the lines of communication between the parents and their physician should always be kept open. I always remind my patients, that, as a physician, I will not be the determinant of your pregnancy and it's outcome, but a helper, an educator, and a well-informed observer.

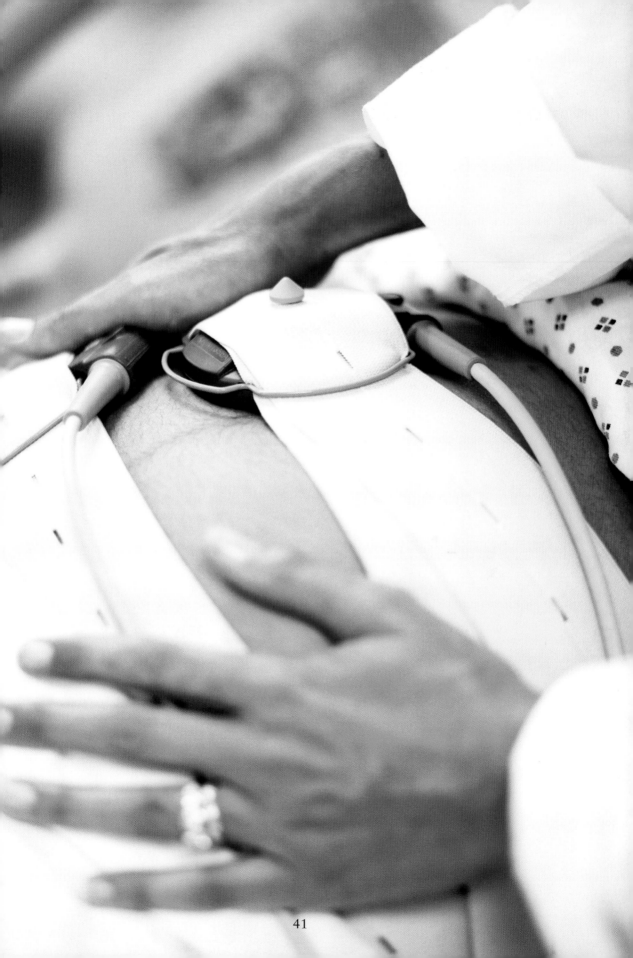

—᧒ 14 ᧒—

5 Things You Must Do
When You Are Pregnant

You'll read the books, talk to other moms-to-be, and watch the evening news. It will seem as if there are a million things that you must do and the list grows longer each day. As your pregnancy progresses, you'll be surprised to learn that many are really optional. The following five, however, are non-negotiable:

1. *Stop smoking. Period.*

2. *Stop drinking alcohol. Period.*

3. *Limit caffeine.*

4. *Drink 8 glasses of water every day.*

5. *Eat healthy and take a prenatal vitamin.*

15

DHA for Y-O-U

You know the benefits of folic acid, but do you know about DHA (docosahexaenoic acid)? DHA is the new wonder supplement that actually increases your baby's brain growth.

It is an "omega-3 fatty acid" found in some foods, including certain fish, fish oils, and seafood. In infants, this nutrient is very important for proper development of the brain and the retina of the eye. Since a baby's brain develops dramatically in the last trimester of pregnancy and in the first three months of life, most infant formula brands have started adding DHA, an important component of breast milk. to their products.

Now, with new supplements on the market, you can boost your own DHA level in your third trimester, when much of the fetus' neurological, visual and nervous system development occurs. If you are nursing your baby, you can continue to boost your DHA in the baby's first three months through your own breast milk if you continue taking DHA supplements.

16

Make Mine A Water

Drinking enough fluids is always important, but much more so during pregnancy. What could be better than pure, clear water? If you drink enough fluids, 8 to 10 full glasses each day, you are less likely to become de-hydrated, constipated, or have urinary infections.

Plus, your baby needs fluids for proper growth. Choose caffeine-free, non-alcoholic drinks like juices, milk, clear soups, and hey - how about a glass of water?

Nutrition REALLY Matters

It's no secret, your nutrition *really matters* while you are pregnant.

The old adage about eating for two has now been borne out by scientific studies that link the roots of diseases, illnesses, and even length of life, all the way back to the womb, and the nutrition of moms-to-be. Low birth weight, which could be caused by too few calories, too little protein, too much fat, or too few vitamins, increases the risks of heart disease and cardiovascular disease later on in life.

Believe it or not, you are actually shaping your baby's entire future health pattern with the nutritional choices you make right now. Don't be alarmed though, good nutrition is not really a mystery. It just takes a little common sense and a little will power to skip the junk food. Do it for your baby, and you will benefit, too.

Pass up the chocolate cake
for something that, perhaps,
grows on a tree.

The

Baby

Made

Me

Eat

It!

18

The New
Pickles And Ice Cream

In a survey of 1,000 pregnant women, the most mentioned food cravings were:

1. Chocolate
2. Potato Chips
3. Tacos
4. Soft Pretzels
5. Popsicles

19

Find Your Sport

Despite the aches and pains, heartburn, and swollen ankles, exercise will make you feel sooo much better.

You don't have to set any Olympic records and you don't have to keep up with anyone else. Fitness is about moving a little more each day, sensibly. Walking is a wonderful way to get your blood moving without stressing any muscles. Maternity Yoga, Pilates, light weights, whatever you prefer. Fitness is another vital factor in the healthy mom equation. Be good to yourself.

Exercise.

One Small Step
For Mom,
One Healthy Leap
For BABY

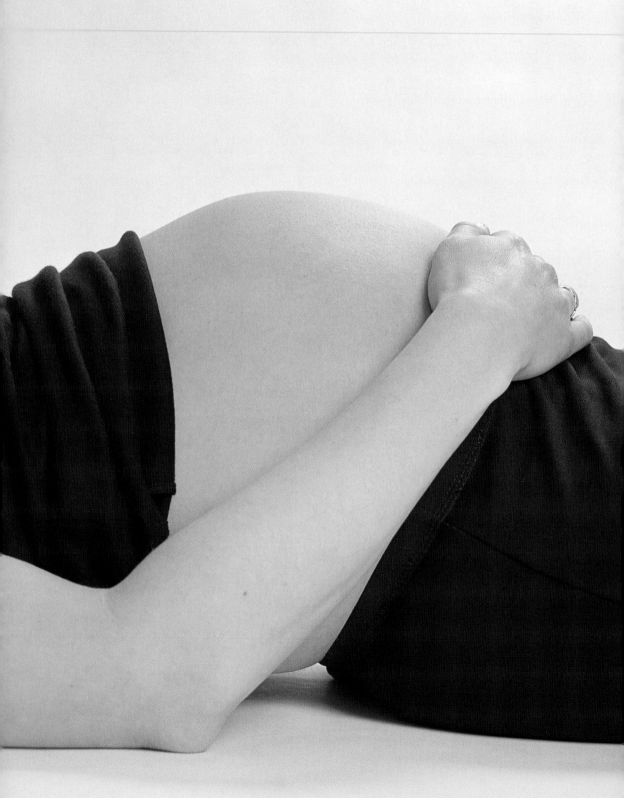

20

Massage The World Away

This just in — you can now get a pre-natal massage.

While pregnancy means giving up some things, you don't have to give up your massage. *Aaaah, that's a relief.* Today, more and more spas are offering certified pre-natal massage. What a great way to relieve stress and help your aching back, legs, neck, or whatever.

Of course, you should be sure your masseuse is specially trained to treat pregnant women, and *always check with your doctor first.* Stay away from foot reflexology, which is a special form of foot massage, because, in some cases, it has been known to induce labor. Otherwise, there is no reason not to indulge in a fabulous, stress-relieving, maternity massage.

~ 21 ~

Rock-A-Bye, Mommy

Simply stated, pregnancy is a time for pampering your-self. One way to accomplish this is to take a nap, every day. Of course, regardless of how tired you are, you will always be able to think of at least a dozen other things you could be doing. Sleep is the best way to rejuvenate a body that is working harder than ever before.

You need more sleep right now, and you may even find that you sleep better when you are pregnant. *(And, I guar-antee, that you won't sleep very well once the baby comes.)* When it comes to pregnancy, nothing is more important than taking care of yourself and your baby, so make the time. Even a 30 minute nap will help get you through the rest of the day, happier.

Pampering yourself is not just a recommendation, but a requirement for your sanity!

DO NOT DISTURB

22

Start Your Scrapbooking, Immediately

You may have bought the obligatory video camera and a few dozen rolls of film to document the big day, but why wait until you're in labor to record the most amazing period of your life.

Start your scrapbook, immediately, by treating yourself to a special scrapbook for your pregnancy. This will make collecting photos, stories, and momentos fun and easy.

While you're at it, start a journal, even if it's only a few sentences each day. You will enjoy remembering the tiny details of this wondrous experience. As your baby grows inside you, your scrapbook and journal will be growing, too. When your baby goes off to college, or gets married, won't this make an awesome present?

23

Move Your Mother Next Door

You've waited your whole life to grow up and strike out on your own, so you may be wondering why I'm suggesting that you move your mother next door.

Well, even if it's just for a week, you WILL need help, and who could be better than your mother? The best part is, almost every mother will see this as a gift rather than a chore, so you get the *two-birds-with-one-stone advantage*.

If your mother is the bossy, domineering type, you can try to limit the visit to a few days or a week, *but don't kick her out until you get a few long naps in the bargain.* If your mother is the easy-to-get-along-with type, roll out the red carpet and you will make out like a bandit!

An ounce of prevention is worth a pound of cure.

—B. Franklin

24

Home, Safe, Home

We baby-proofed our house, but they kept getting in anyway!

Just kidding, parenting is really going to be fun! But you do need to do some serious baby-proofing *while you are pregnant.* There won't be time to do much of anything after the baby arrives. You won't believe how those babies can get into places and things that you would never have thought about when you were childless and carefree.

Pack up your valuable glass knick-knacks and your mother's antique vase, or at least put them up very, very high. Then, crawl around on the floor. You'll be amazed at how many things you can find that would hurt you if you were 10 months old and putting everything you got your hands on into your mouth. Finally, get rid of all sharp and dangerous objects and lock cabinets containing medicines and cleaning products.

Pregnancy and motherhood have given me the direct experience of divine intelligence. I remember the moment I realized I was pregnant. I felt the presence of spirit inside me. I wondered where I had come from and I felt the surge of the creative impulse of the universe bursting through me. Time stood still and I felt connected to eternity.

I visualized the baby that was growing inside of me, and started to whisper little secrets of love to her. I felt a soul inside of me, a soul that was innocent and pure and powerful, and listened to my thoughts and to the joy and love in my heart.

When I saw my baby for the first time, I cried tears of joy at the miracle before me. Her ten tiny fingers and toes, her perfect features, her search for my smell, my touch, and my voice — a divine presence, beautiful, holy and sacred. Through my child, the world around me sparkled in a new light. I was able to see miracles at every turn - the miracle of nature, relationships, and love.

And with each day, my love for my child grows. It is a love that I had never experienced before — a love with no expectations, unbounded, pure, tender, completely vulnerable and with no defenses. I have gotten to know my baby as her own individual. She disarms me with her unique smile, cooing in her own language, and blissfully taking in the world around her. I fall in love with her over and over again.

With my second pregnancy, I was nervous that I would never love another being in the way that I had loved my first child. But, I soon realized that love has no boundaries. My love for my daughter only fueled the love for my second baby. Love is the essence of spirit and grows stronger with each expression of attention, appreciation and affection.

I thank my daughters for teaching me the real meaning of spirituality. They have taught me what it feels like to be vulnerable, powerful and defenseless. They teach me about the miracles of our existence through the wonder in their eyes and the innocence of their blissful laughter. They have shown me the power of unconditional love. It radiates from their being like light from a bonfire in all directions. It brings back joy and laughter from wherever it is reflected.

⁓ 25 ⁓

The Five Greatest Things About Being Pregnant

So much attention is given to the somewhat annoying aspects of pregnancy, that the benefits are often overlooked. While there are certainly more than five great things about pregnancy, these five top the list.

1. *You get to eat more.*

2. *People give you their seat in public places.*

3. *You have an interior heater that keeps you warm in the winter.*

4. *You don't get your period for nine months.*

5. *Cleavage!*

~ 26 ~
Motherhood Is Hot

That's right, Motherhood *Is* HOT. Don't allow yourself to think dowdy when you are pregnant. You are more attractive now, than ever.

For some of us, we will have cleavage for the first *and only time!* You are oh, so sexy to your husband now, so bask in the glow and don't be afraid to show off a few curves.

A pregnant body is a beautiful body and you should never be uncomfortable about how you look.

The connection between the mind, body, and spirit is powerful. Looking good will have a lasting, positive effect on your mind and spirit.

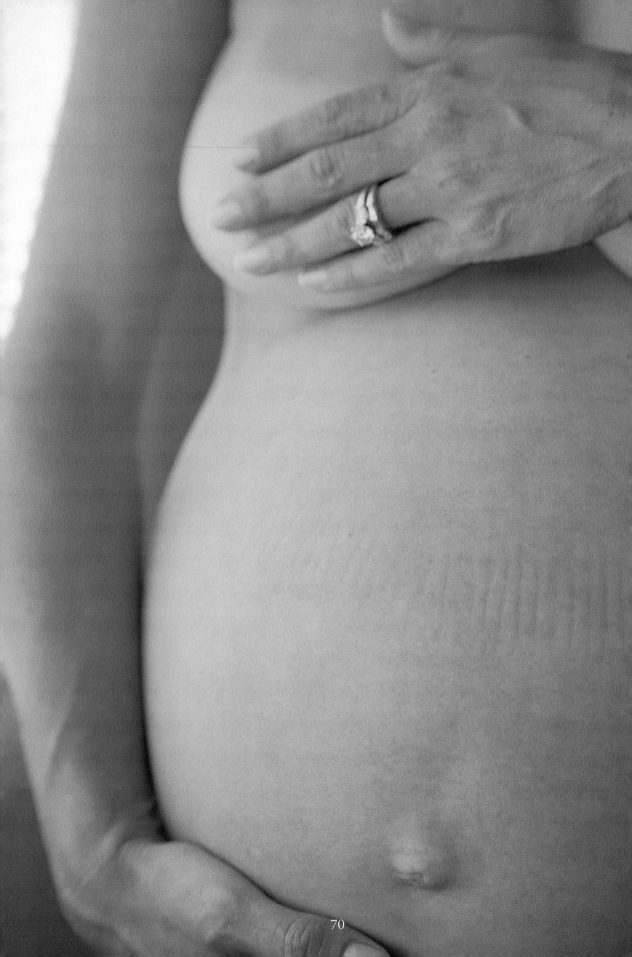

27

Sexy, Inside And Out

The most important part of your maternity wardrobe? Sexy lingerie, including a great bra.

Combine a need, *more support as your breasts grow,* and a want, *to be sexy and desirable,* into a fun purchase: sexy, maternity lingerie. I, personally, think it should be the first article of maternity clothing that you buy. Just make sure your bra fits correctly and has plenty of support, keeping in mind that a little lace couldn't hurt!

You may be surprised to know that the thong has reached the maternity world. It will make you feel fabulous to be wearing a secret underneath — *sexy lingerie.*

28

The "New" Happy Hour

Sure, everyone knows you shouldn't drink alcohol while you are pregnant, but there's no reason to sit at home while your friends are having a night out on the town. You can still go bar-hopping if you have a list of cool, non-alcoholic drinks at the ready. Starting with a Virgin Mary, for obvious reasons, my favorite drink for pregnant women, here is my list:

1. Virgin Mary — *it comes with that cool celery stick*
2. Frozen Virgin Margarita — *ask for the umbrella*
3. Virgin Pina Colada — *say the word "virgin" with attitude*
4. Virgin Bay Breeze — *you can almost smell the salt air*
5. Non-alcoholic Beer — *tastes great, safe for your baby*

And, of course,
don't forget to toast!

May the best of your yesterdays,
be the worst of your tomorrows...

Some women feel that the remedy to a maternity body is to purchase bigger clothing.

Unfortunately, this will not work because these new clothes will be too big all over your body.

29

The Greatest Shopping Excuse, EVER!

There's more to pregnancy than morning sickness and the bathroom relay. Grab a friend and start shopping!

Do you need any more justification to indulge yourself? A pregnant woman is like the woman whose house has just burned down. She actually "has nothing to wear." *While this is something I tend to say almost every morning,* lucky you — in your case it's really true! Nothing fits and you are obligated to shop.

The great, big secret is that maternity clothes have come a long way since your mother was pregnant, and you are going to be amazed at how great you will look and feel in your new maternity wardrobe.

30

A Little Known Fact

Here is a little-known, secret benefit of pregnancy — it reduces your risk of developing ovarian cancer.

Ovarian cancer is the fifth most common form of cancer in women, with an estimated 25,400 women expected to develop this illness, each year. The incessant ovulation theory speculates that uninterrupted ovulation causes repeated trauma to the ovary, and eventually can lead to ovarian cancer. Women who are pregnant "interrupt" the string of ovulations. Their risk of ovarian cancer is lower than that of women who were never pregnant. Even better for those dreaming of a large family, this protective effect increases with each pregnancy.

*Mother Nature
meant for you to
get pregnant!*

31

FREE STUFF!

You see it on the news and you hear it from everyone who has a child - kids cost money, big money. The one thing, however, that you don't often hear is that a lot of people will want to give you free stuff.

You may not realize it, but as a pregnant woman, you have just become one of the most sought after consumers in the country. Once the baby arrives, you will be buying a multitude of things, starting with diapers, baby clothes, and baby food, as you progress to that new stroller, crib, and baby seat. You may even be in the market for a mini van and possibly a bigger house.

Everyone will be courting you, so play the field! *This is the one time you may want to be on everyone's mailing list,* because they want to send you free stuff. Samples, coupons, gifts with purchase, you name it. You have become very popular and since you will be buying a variety of products, you might as well get your share of free stuff!

Motherhood, The Soundtrack

The good news is that a recent study suggests an expectant mother's calm, stress-free feelings will be transmitted to her baby. The bad news is that, during pregnancy, finding the right words to explain your feelings and the intensity of your emotions is often difficult.

Luckily, some very talented singers and songwriters have used songs to capture the hopes, dreams, and emotions of pregnancy and parenthood. So put on some soothing music, take a deep breath, and relax. You just may find yourself singing one of these songs while your little one hums along!

The Most Requested Songs
Of Mothers And Mothers-To-Be

A Mother's Prayer — **Celine Dion**

Beautiful Boy — **Celine Dion**

I Hope You Dance — **Lee Ann Womack**

Isn't She Lovely — **Stevie Wonder**

Just The Two Of Us — **Will Smith**

Return To Pooh Corner — **Kenny Loggins**

Close To You — **The Carpenters**

Danny's Song — **Loggins and Messina**

Butterfly Kisses — **Bob Carlisle**

Daddy's Little Girl

Lullabye - Goodnight, My Angel — **Billy Joel**

Father and Daughter — **Paul Simon**

If I Could — **Regina Belle**

～ 32 ～

The Five Worst Things About Being Pregnant

Of course, we all know about the worst parts of pregnancy, but they pale in comparison to the magic of creating a new life. On the bright side, it will all be over soon! You'll feel better to know that the following are the five worst things about pregnancy:

1. *Swollen feet and ankles.*

2. *Heartburn - always carry mints.*

3. *Having to go to the bathroom about 50 times a day (make sure you always know where the closest one is).*

4. *Not being able to ski, skydive, ride horses, etc. This won't be the last sacrifice you make for your child.*

5. *Not being able to tie your shoes.*

Morning Sickness All Day Long

This is a big mystery to me. Why is it called morning sickness? Nausea and vomiting can occur at any time during the day, but usually it only lasts for the first three or four months of your pregnancy. It is associated with the increase in your hormone levels. Some women have told me that bubbly water, or cola calms their stomachs down a little, while the use of ginger is also recommended. My sister always carried mints or gum to fight morning sickness and the bad taste that went along with it.

Your own appetite will tell you to stay away from greasy or spicy foods. Stick with small portions of bland foods, and try crackers or toast as a snack.

Of course, tell your doctor if your morning sickness is severe, or includes a fever. Just remember, this too shall pass.

⚛ 34 ⚛

Swollen Feet, Stretch Marks, Red Eyes, Oh My!

You are about to learn what true beauty is. Swollen feet, stretch marks, and red eyes sound slightly less than glamorous, but they are a small price to pay for the miracle you are about to experience.

While you'd probably be just as happy if you could send them packing, don't despair! Today's expectant mothers have an arsenal of products and secrets to help relieve and reduce these little nuisances.

Drinking plenty of water, getting enough rest, keeping your feet up, and a little moisturizer can do wonders. Whether you are in the midst of first trimester nausea or three days overdue, you are still attractive and sexy, both inside and out. Remember - you have "inner beauty" now and all the world can see it.

~ 35 ~

You're Not Overweight, You're Pregnant

During your pregnancy, it's okay *and natural* to get big —you're not overweight, you're pregnant.

Regardless of how much you used to weigh, you will now weigh more. While this is not rocket science, you'd be amazed at how many pregnant women lose sight of this simple fact. Your doctor will tell you how much is too much weight to gain. Your job is to eat healthy, and not let your self-image turn negative because your abdomen, *and maybe a few other places,* have expanded.

Focus on the important things in life: a healthy baby and a happy mom. Let *your baby's pounds and ounces be the only weight you think about.*

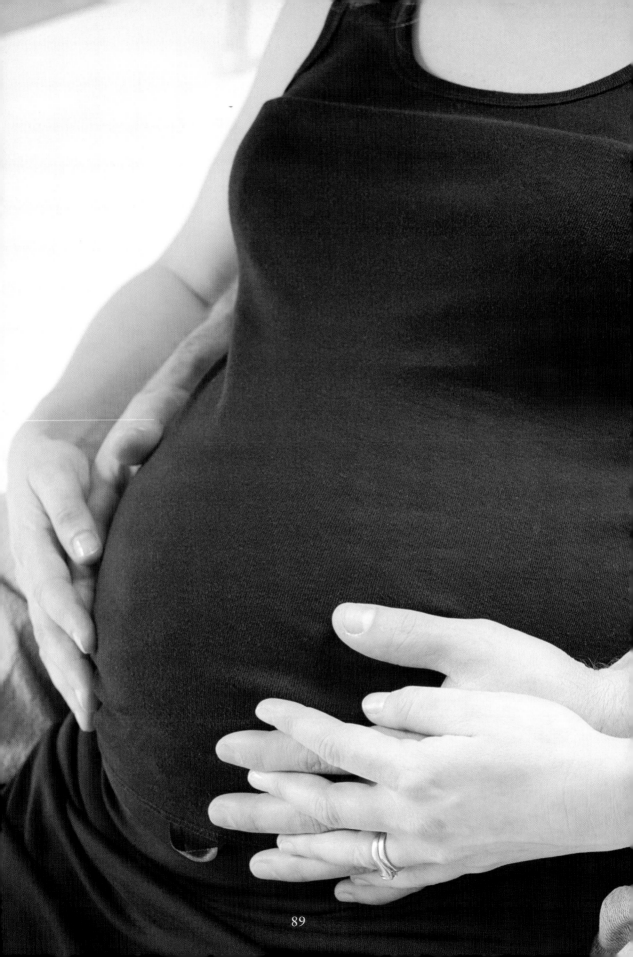

Thinking sexy,
not size,

is the first step to
looking sexy.

36

You Have No Idea How Big You're Going To Get

I'm not saying this to alarm you, only to prepare you. I just want you to be ready. Go to a maternity store and try on the maternity "pillow" that they keep in the fitting room. It is meant to add three months to your pregnancy size.

Now see if that safety pin that is holding your jeans closed still works. I didn't think so! I'll tell you a secret: you'll probably need to buy a few maternity outfits, and you may not want to wait until the last minute. Think ahead.

Today's maternity fashions *are comfortable, flattering, and will improve your self-confidence and mood. Maintaining your pre-pregnancy style is much easier than you think!*

❧ 37 ❧

Weighing In

I was curious about how much weight women really do gain in their pregnancy, so I asked them! In a survey of one thousand pregnant women, here is how much weight they have gained

	1st Trimester	2nd Trimester	3rd Trimester
0-9 lbs	91%	58%	15%
10-19 lbs	7%	31%	30%
20-29 lbs	2%	9%	27%
30-39 lbs		2%	21%
40-49 lbs			5%
over 50 lbs			2%

What have we learned from this? There is a wide range of how much weight women gain, and as long as you follow your doctor's advice, you are in good company!

The beauty of a pregnant woman
cannot be measured on a scale,
...especially a bathroom scale!

Twinkle, twinkle

little star,

How I

wonder

who you are.

Counting days

until we

meet

and

I can kiss

your cheek

so sweet.

~⚬ 38 ⚬~

Myth Or Fact: Boy Or Girl?

By your fifth month, you may find yourself resting comfortably, only to look up and see an anxious aunt dangling a ring on a chain over your stomach. Don't worry, this is just an old wives' tales used to determine the sex of your baby. And, there are plenty more where that came from:

You're definitely having a boy if your legs are hairier than they're ever been before. You're definitely having a girl if you develop a craving for sweets. If you're carrying high and up front, it's a boy, but carrying all around is definitely a girl.

Should you have an ultrasound and find out for sure? Or should you just be surprised on the big day? Maybe you'll find out but keep it a big secret. Your husband really wants a boy and you need to know whether to paint the nursery pink or blue. Of course, if you decide to find out early, you should keep in mind that an ultrasound doesn't always get it right.

So, let me straighten you out on this great big secret. Sit back, relax and get ready to celebrate your boy or your girl (or if you're doubly blessed...both). Next question?

~ 39 ~

Month Nine Nesting

Whether it's folklore, or scientific fact, there's something to the old 'nesting instinct'. When it hits you, take advantage of it.

Your instincts are on the money by wanting to tie up loose ends and straighten out the closets. You will thank yourself when the baby comes and you have room for baby food, diapers, baby gear, etc. The next time you clean between the cracks in the bathroom tiles might just be years away, as busy as you'll be with the new baby.

What about getting your address book updated? When it's time to send thank you cards for baby presents, it can be quite frustrating to dig through a shoebox full of addresses with a screaming newborn on your lap.

A little organization now, can save a lot of frustration later!

Nursing Your Baby Is Good For YOU

Everyone knows that nursing is good for your baby. Mother's milk is the perfect nutritional food for newborns, and your baby receives important antibodies and nutrients from you.

But, did you know that nursing your baby, even for a short amount of time, will reduce your odds of getting breast cancer later in life? Or, that nursing will help you get back in shape quicker, help you bond with your baby and "turn you into a mom" more easily?

If you aren't completely sure about nursing your baby, give it some serious consideration.

~ 41 ~

B.Y.O.B.
Bring Your Own Bottle

While many new moms are quite comfortable nursing their babies, breastfeeding is not for everyone. Keep in mind, that if you don't breastfeed your baby, *you are not a bad mother*.

This decision is to be made by you, after consulting with your husband and your doctor. Period. It should never be a decision based upon social pressures or comparisons with family and friends.

There are many valid reasons not to nurse, if you so choose. Bottle-feeding allows dad to participate in the experience *(especially at 1am)*, and some moms may simply choose the extra freedom that comes with bottlefeeding.

This is America. We have the freedom of choice, so exercise yours, without regret.

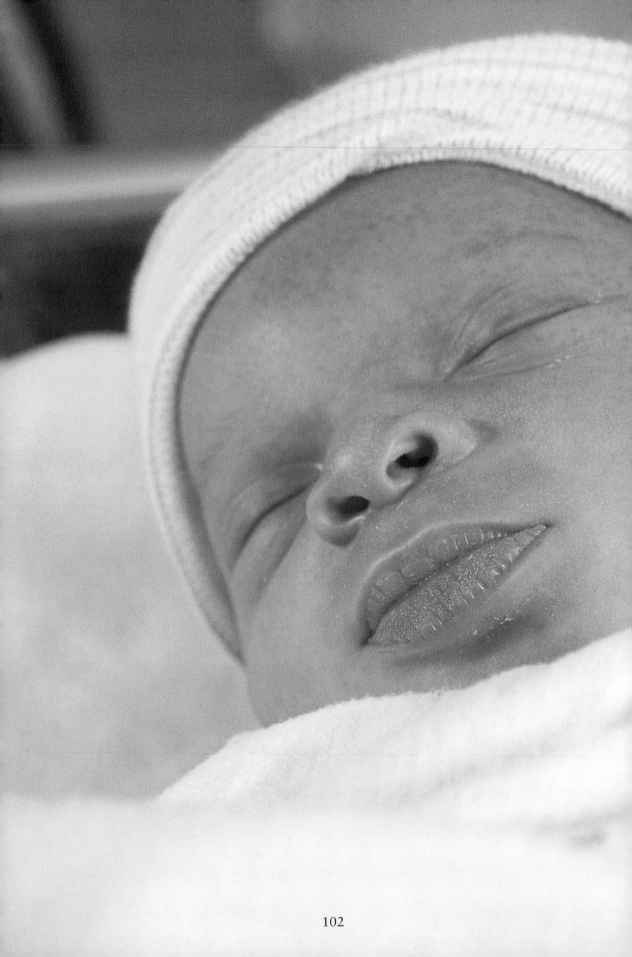

42

Your Baby's Secret Weapon

You probably haven't given it much thought, but your baby has a secret weapon that might prove very helpful one day: *cord blood*.

Cord blood is the blood in the umbilical cord connecting you to your baby. It is rich in stem cells, which are the "beginning building blocks" for all of the other cells and tissues that make up your body.

Recently, scientists have been able to use stem cells from one family member to fight and even cure some diseases in other family members. These cells hold promise, in the future, to prevent and cure many illnesses, such as cancer, heart disease, and Alzheimer's.

A new industry has begun which, for a fee, collects the cord blood which is present at birth, during your baby's delivery, and preserves it for potential use later. You may want to find out more about this procedure and discuss it with your doctor. After all, it is a one-time decision that cannot be repeated.

∽ 43 ∽

Most Common
Secret Fears

*In a survey of 1,000 pregnant women,
the most common secret fears were:*

42% My baby will have some type of a birth defect.

27% I won't lose the weight after the baby is born.

16% Labor and delivery will be painful.

9% I won't be a good mom.

2% My husband will be unfaithful while I'm pregnant.

I'm thrilled to know there is such trust among pregnant women in their husbands!

∽ 44 ∾

There's No Such Thing As A New Fear

Pregnancy can be equal parts exciting and scary. While you may be afraid to verbalize your own secret fears, you should know that it is perfectly normal to have some. You would be amazed at how many women have the same secret fears!

We asked 1,000 pregnant women to share their secret fears of pregnancy with us. It may be reassuring to know that there is nothing "off limits". In no particular order, some of the secret fears mentioned included:

1. *I will die in childbirth.*
2. *My baby will get tangled in the cord.*
3. *I will drop my baby.*
4. *I won't be able to handle the new responsibilities.*

It helps to get your secret fears out into the open. Ask your doctor, confide in your mother or a friend, or write them down. *Then stop worrying.*

45

This Won't Hurt A Bit

I'm actually surprised when I hear from newly pregnant women that one of their greatest secret fears is pain during labor and delivery.

After all, this is the 21st Century and we do have drugs and painkillers. So, why feel that you need to be a hero and go solo? Would you go to the dentist and refuse novocaine? Everyone has their own pain tolerance level and only you know yours.

There have been millions of babies born with the aid of painkillers and, if you so desire, your baby can be one of them. Let's permanently eliminate this secret, unnecessary fear. Besides, you have other things to worry about, *like what to wear to your baby shower.*

Where's The Stork When You Need Him?

Fear of the unknown is the greatest cause of stress during pregnancy, labor, & delivery.

46

What Are The Odds?

Fear of birth defects is clearly the number one fear uncovered by our survey, so let's look at the facts. According to the March of Dimes, whose mission is to improve the health of babies by preventing birth defects and infant mortality, each year about 150,000 babies are born with birth defects. Since there are just over 4 million births in the United States each year, this translates into 3.75% of births.

What can you do to improve the odds? First and foremost, is prenatal health care visits with your doctor, including a "pre-pregnancy" visit to uncover medical problems. Daily multi-vitamins, including folic acid, are an absolute must. Of course, a woman who is pregnant or planning pregnancy should avoid alcohol, smoking, and street drugs, all of which can cause birth defects.

While some birth defects are genetic and cannot be *prevented,* The March of Dimes provides a wealth of information on their website, www.marchofdimes.com. Do all you can to have a healthy baby and then, when your baby is born, you will love him or her regardless of shape, size, or condition.

March *of* Dimes
Saving babies, together®

∽ 47 ∾

Myth or Fact:
Stay Away From Cats

There are plenty of old wives' tales about pregnant women and cats. You don't have to give away your kitty while you are pregnant, but you do need to exercise some good sense.

The danger in cats is that cat feces can sometimes cause a parasite called *Toxoplasma Gondi*, which could harm your baby. The parasite can penetrate the placenta and enter the fetal circulation implanting in the fetal brain causing significant damage to the fetal central nervous system. Typically outside cats are those that are infected, due to their contact with infected mice. Most likely, mothers who have been exposed to cats prior to pregnancy stand a good chance of having been previously exposed to the parasite and have made protective antibodies. An antibody test may be performed before the patient becomes pregnant to determine her susceptibility. If she is found to be protected, she can interact more closely with the cat.

Naturally, the best course of action, is to let someone else change the litter box, and wash your hands thoroughly after holding your cat. *While you're at it, you may want to prepare "Fluffy" for the new little love in your life.*

~ 48 ~

Leave Your Master Plan
At The Door

You have been planning for this baby for a long time. Your husband wants a boy so he can take him to little league and build a tree house. You have already made play dates for your delicate ballerina with your best friend's new baby. You've planned out everything from the labor and delivery to the brand of diapers and future hobbies.

Well, unfortunately, your baby has had nine months to make his or her own plan. You will be shocked to find out how different it can be from yours!

Your special breathing techniques for L&D may turn into an emergency C-section. Your boy might be a girl, or a boy who hates little league and has a fear of heights *(there goes the tree house)*. Even worse, your ballerina might hate ballet and not get along with your best friend's baby! So just relax and expect the unexpected. With babies, you learn to take *and cherish* what you get and say thank you.

What's In A Name?

Choosing your baby's name is a fun time. There certainly are a lot of choices! Just pick up any of the baby naming books at the bookstore and settle in for the evening. But, before you make up your mind, make sure you will still love the name you choose, 20 years from now. You'll be saying it about 100 times a day.

And please, check out the initials. Let's not have an unfortunate acronym spelled out on the monogrammed receiving blanket.

Speaking of names, here's a fun fact: According to the Social Security Administration, the top baby names for boy and girl, in the decade 1900-1910, were John and Mary. In the decade 1990 to 2000, the top names were Michael and Ashley.

~ 50 ~

Trust Your Instincts

You may have heard a rumor that babies don't arrive with instructions or a maintenance manual and unfortunately, it's true. Parenting is all about on-the-job-training, even though many people will insist on giving you unsolicited advice. They mean well, but take heart, you are going to become your own expert on raising your baby faster than you can imagine.

Trust your own instincts! Learn to believe half of what you hear from Aunt Joan or your best friend.

Ultimately, when it comes to your child, you should trust your instincts.
They're much stronger than you know.

~ 51 ~

It Takes A Lifetime To Become A Mother

It takes a minute to conceive a child, but a lifetime to become a mother. The fact is, motherhood is a journey, not a destination. The moment your baby is born you will be mom, but you will have to grow into that title.

One minute you are the patient in the maternity ward, being pampered, the center of attention, on the receiving end. The next minute you are doing all of the giving, all of the worrying, and all of the pampering as your baby takes center stage. This is not an easy transition and it doesn't necessarily come right away.

I remember the first day home as a new mom, feeling sore, and tired, and in need of tender loving care. But instead of being the patient, I had to be the nurse! When your baby cries at 1am and needs to eat and have a diaper change, you are the one doing the work, *even though all you really want is to have your own mother smooth your forehead, and bring you chicken soup, as you roll over and go back to sleep.*

But here's the secret: there is no greater joy in life than giving love and care to your child. It's that simple. It may take you some time to appreciate this, but as you stare lovingly at your newborn, as you burst with pride when he/she takes that first step, as you cry tears of joy when she/he graduates from nursery school, grade school, high school, and college, you will suddenly remember your own mother's smile at similar moments. That's when you'll get it. That's when you'll understand the secrets of motherhood. Your mother may have tried to tell you, but you can't really hear it until you are a mother yourself.

Welcome to the
Secret Society of Motherhood.

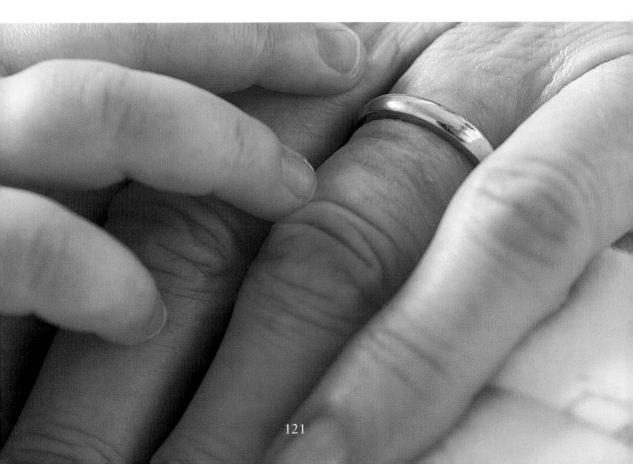

To New Moms, From New Moms

You can read all of the books and visit all of the sites, but more often than not, the most useful information is just a 'mom' away. As a mother of three myself, I believe that there is no substitute for the experiences mothers generously share.

This section was inspired by the questions I hear from expectant mothers each week. The advice, however, comes from a group of esteemed, world-renowned experts — other new moms!

I found that the tricks of the mommy trade that worked were different as my tribe increased. With baby number one the life-saver was in re-arranging my home to have everything within easy reach. This was for two reasons: 1. I was too sore to reach high, or bend low. Squatting to get the dog food was simply not an option. 2. I was doing everything one-handed with a wailing colicky infant.

After baby number four, when I (unfortunately) had legs like bridge cables and cat-like reflexes, the most valuable practice became taking a mid-morning or afternoon cat-nap to build up a little sleep cushion. Sleep is like money in the bank. The less you have the more stressed you are likely to become!

LISA SUHAY, Mother of 4 boys and the author of 5 children's books, including: *There Goes a Mermaid! A NorFolktale* which benefits the Virginian-Pilot Joy Fund and The Literacy Partnership. www.theliteracypartnership.org

Prepare to give up your old life, prepare to give up sleep, prepare to give up a clean and perfect house and prepare to give up your heart completely.

MIMI ROGERS, Actror, Mother of 2

As much as you don't want to tear yourself away from your baby, for even a minute, let alone an entire evening or day....DO IT! It's so important to take a little time for yourself (take a bath, a walk, have lunch with a friend). AND, take some time each week to spend alone with your spouse. Go to a movie or dinner or whatever you can squeeze in. You'll feel refreshed, rejuvenated and love your baby even more when you get back to him/her.

CATHERINE BELL,
Star of the long-running television series,
JAG, Mother of 1, Gemma

Before your baby is born, interview babysitters, set aside one night every week or every other week, and get out with your husband. You will never feel like you have the time, so you really have to force yourself to make the time. Once you get out, you'll be glad you did.

ELLIE, Dallas, TX
Secretary, Mother of 2

Be realistic! Having a baby will be the most wonderful, frustrating, thrilling, terrifying experience you'll ever encounter. If you don't expect the fairy tale, you'll do just fine. And, have a sense of humor. When the lid flies off of the bottle you're vigorously shaking, what else can you do, but laugh?

BARBARA, Long Island, NY
Teacher, Mother of 2

Every new mom should cut herself some slack. While you get used to your new role, laundry and dishes will pile up, more meals will require a can opener, and the day will end before you have a moment to get a morning shower. Despite all of that, it unfortunately, goes by too fast.

MAUREEN, Baltimore, MD, Waitress, Mother of twins, age 2

The best thing I ever did while pregnant, was to listen to my sister-in-law and put my daughter, Nina, on a schedule from day one. A schedule of feeding, playtime and sleeptime rotated throughout the day and night. *(No playtime at night.)* Within a few weeks, I could set the clock by Nina... I knew exactly when I could go to the market, shower and even take a nap myself! She was an extreemly happy baby because all of her needs were being met before she had to make a peep! *(Read the book,* On Becoming Babywise *by Gary Ezzo)*

Also, make sure you get a nightlight for the baby's room so that you don't have to turn on any lights to have a nighttime feeding. Easier on your eyes and to get the baby back to sleep

PERI POLONI, Placerville, CA
Book designer and owner of Knockout Design, www.knockoutbooks.com, Mother of 1

During your pregnancy, laugh a lot...make beautiful sounds for your baby. I bought a CD player with speakers for my tummy, so that my babies could hear the beautiful sounds of Mozart and other great classics.

MARCIA GAY HARDEN,
Actor, Mother of 3,
Eulala Grace, 6, and twins, Hudson
& Julitta Dee, 7 months

Pregnancy is filled with unbelievable joy, happy anticipation, and frequent unsolicited advice. Listen patiently, smile politely, and don't let anyone scare you. You don't need to read every book and watch every video. You're more ready than you know!

LISA FUNARI WILLEVER,
Author and Mother of 2

Start dividing the responsibilities and delegating before the baby comes. It took me nine months to teach my husband how to cook, clean and do laundry!

LORRAINE, Buena Park, CA
Accountant, Mother of 3

Be sure to teach your children about appreciation such as 'thank you for making dinner' or 'thank you for taking me to school' or 'thank you for helping me with my homework'. Acknowledgement to the parent or parents make a big difference. Also, don't forget your spouse, go on weekly dates, make it happen. It only takes two hours for dinner and another hour for a little lovin'!

MARLEE MATLIN, Actor, Mother of 4,
Sarah, 9, Brandon, 4, Tyler, 2, and Isabelle, 1

Nothing will be as soothing to your baby as the sound of your voice or rocking in your arms.

Your Own Secrets

*The best secrets are those shared
between friends.*

A Secret About Rebecca Matthias

FROM **LISA WILLEVER,** THE PUBLISHER

Hi, this is Lisa Willever and my company, Franklin Mason Press is the publisher of this book. As you reach the end, it seems only appropriate to share a well-kept secret about the esteemed author, who herself, has been a well-kept secret. Professionally, she is the woman behind **Mimi Maternity®, A Pea In The Pod®,** and **Motherhood® Maternity,** as well as the largest maternity clothing manufacturer in the world.

But who is Rebecca Matthias? I guess it's time to blow her cover... she's funny — even when she isn't trying to be, she's intelligent — knowing more about numbers than should be legal, and she's real, just ask her husband, Dan and their three children. She is also one of those unique people who not only believes in a cause, but she acts on behalf of it.

In 1999, Rebecca wrote a book entitled *MothersWork®, How A Young Mother Started A Multi-Million Dollar Company On A Shoe String.* In addition to telling her story, she wanted to make a difference. Believing that a chain of business successes would be created if established businesses would guide new companies, she had an idea. She invited all new companies to submit a business plan for her review. There would be one prize and she would select the winner, based upon the strength of the plan.

As a small, new publisher, on the verge of releasing our first title, I nervously entered my company into her contest. In August 2000, we received the phone call of a lifetime, as Rebecca named us best New Business Start-Up and awarded us $10,000.00, from her own personal funds. In addition, and much more valuable, she would serve as our advisor for a period of one year. Well, one year turned into four years and as a result, that first book has turned into thirteen, mostly children's, books, with more on the way.

With virtually no publicity surrounding the contest, it became clear that this was a mission. That's right, other than my family, I doubt anyone even knew about it! Can you imagine giving away $10,000.00 and not getting on the local news? But, that's the point. It is a rare person, especially in Rebecca's position, that would give away a large sum of money and take the time to meet with a growing company, for the sole purpose of guidance and encouragement.

Rebecca Matthias is one of those rare people and if her recent appearance on Oprah is any indication, her days of working behind the scenes are numbered. If there is one thing the world needs right now, its more women like Rebecca to provide us with inspiration, determination, and let's face it, her gorgeous maternity clothes!

As a mother of two myself, it has been an honor to team-up with her to create this book *(although it's been even more fun to share her secret)*! Enjoy the book and your own journey into Motherhood!

LISA M. WILLEVER, Franklin Mason Press